apple

cat

bat

fan

flag

pan

stamp

lamp

long a

table

acorn

baby

paper

long a (final e signal)

grapes

cake

snake

rake

whale

skates

tape

ar (vowel with r)

car

shark

yarn

star

jar

scarf

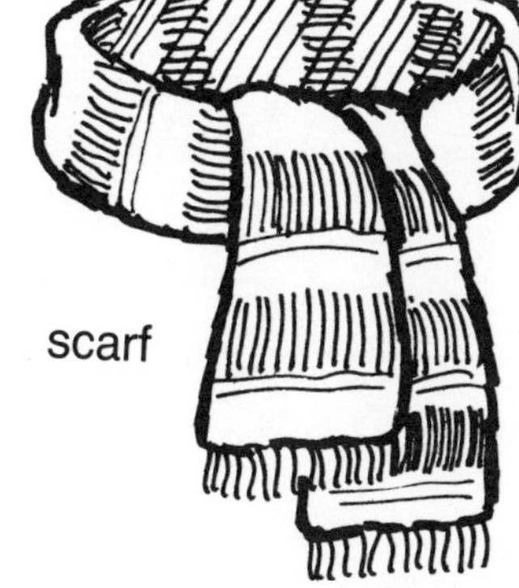

---

al (variant vowel)

ball

wall

salt

---

wa (variant vowel)

watch

swan

water

aw (vowel digraph)

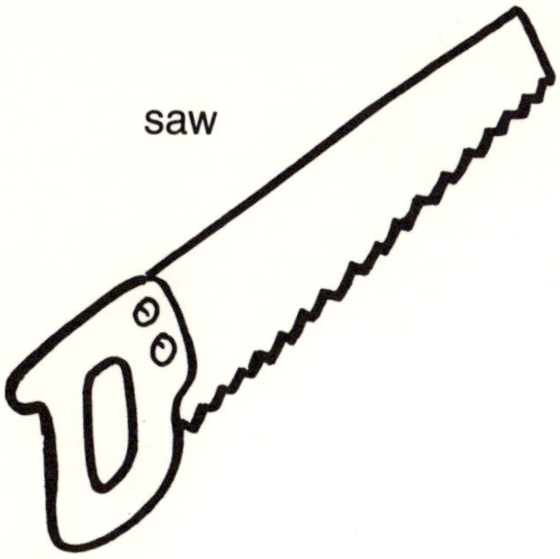

saw

fawn

squawk

au (vowel digraph)

faucet

laundromat

astronaut

ai (long a sound)

snail

pail

train

sailboat

rain

mailbox

ay (long a sound)

clay

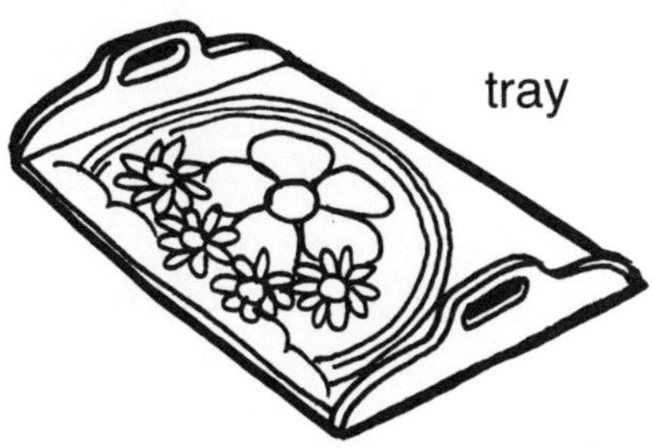

tray

haystack

air (r-modified)

chair

hair

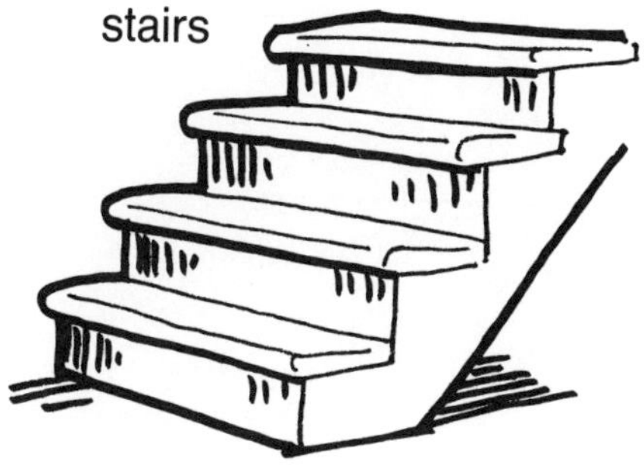

stairs

fair

fairy

are (r-modified)

scare

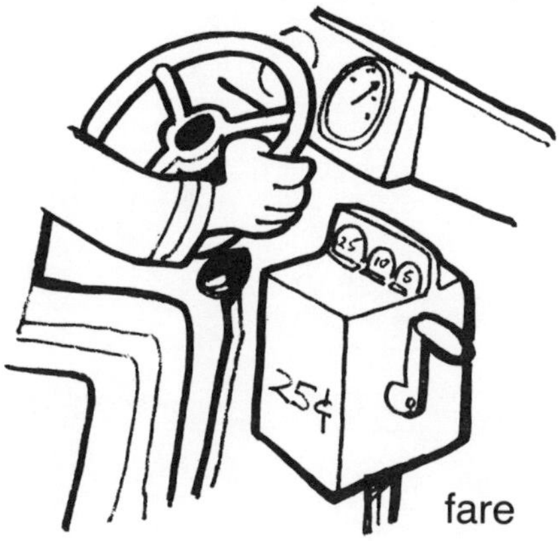

fare

square

initial b

bear

butterfly

bird

book

bell

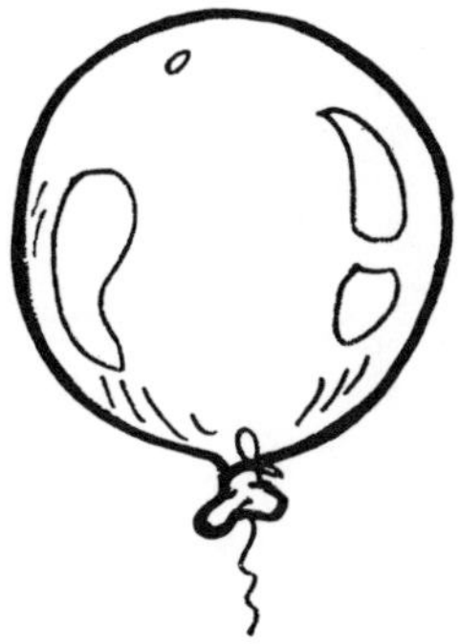

balloon

basket

---

bl blend

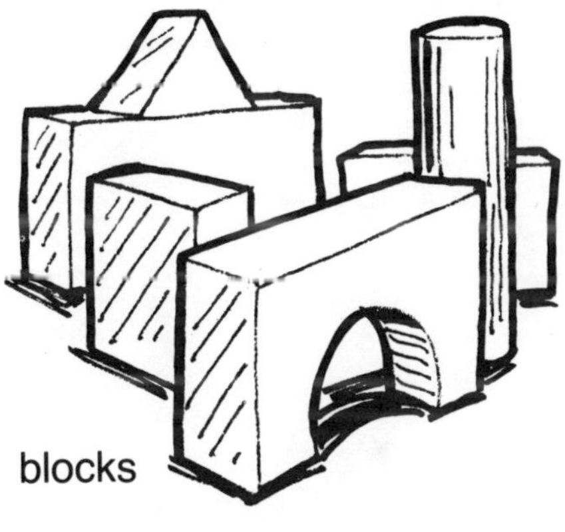

blocks

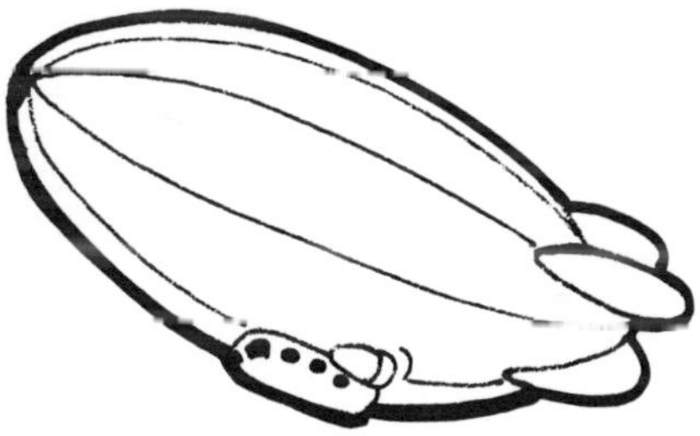

blimp

blanket

---

br blend

broom

bridge

bread

initial hard c

cow

candle
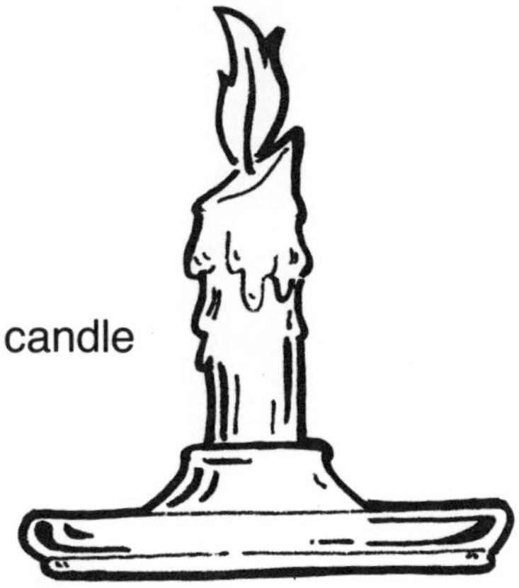

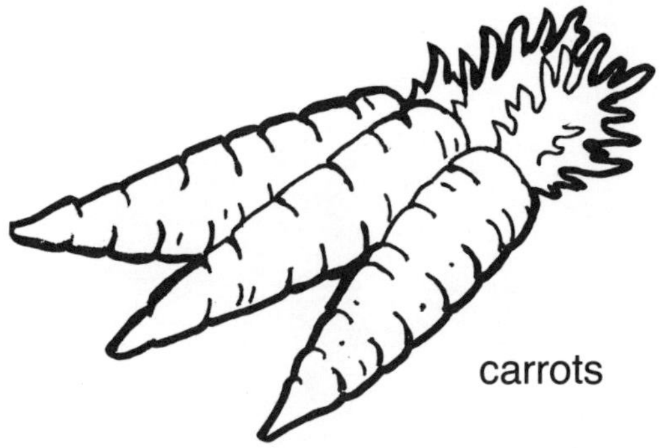
carrots

camera

camel

cactus
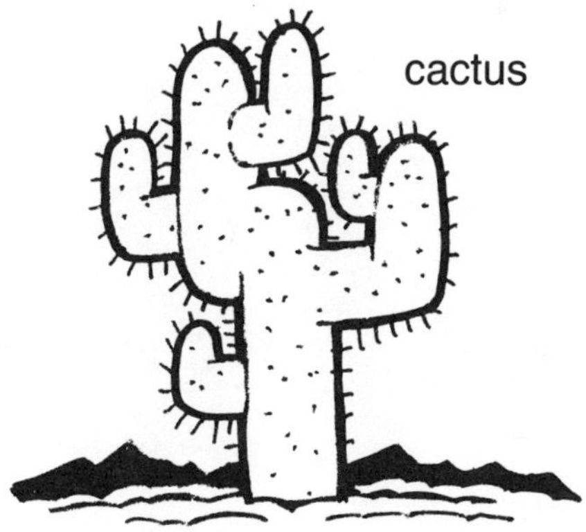

cup

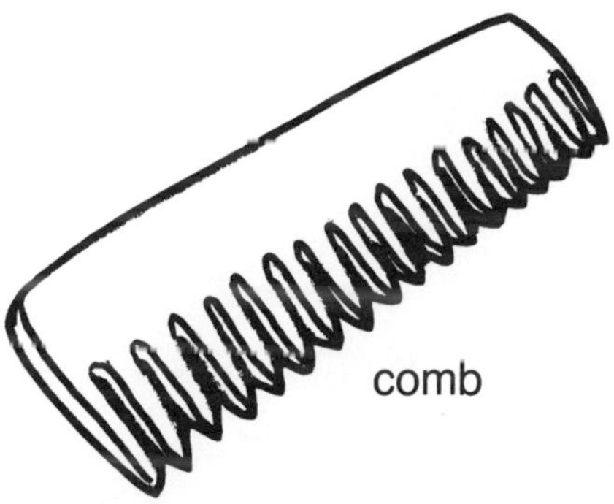
comb

castle

initial soft c

city

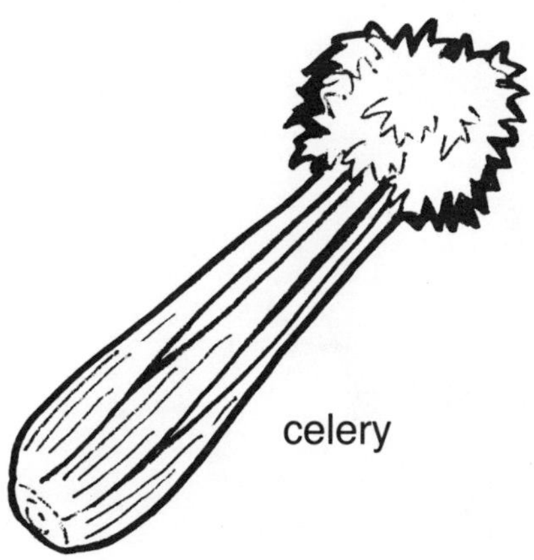
celery

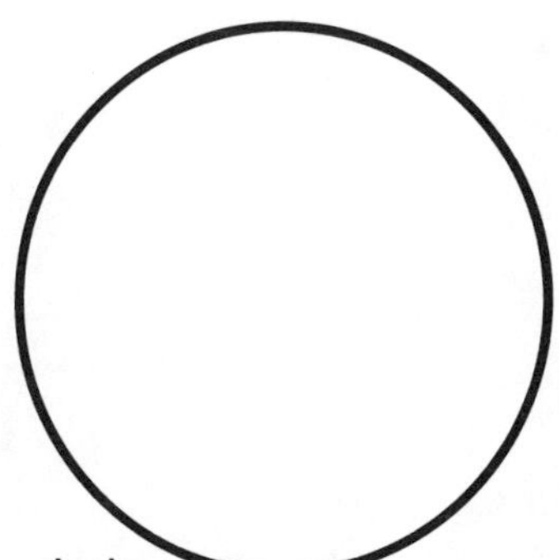
circle

ch digraph

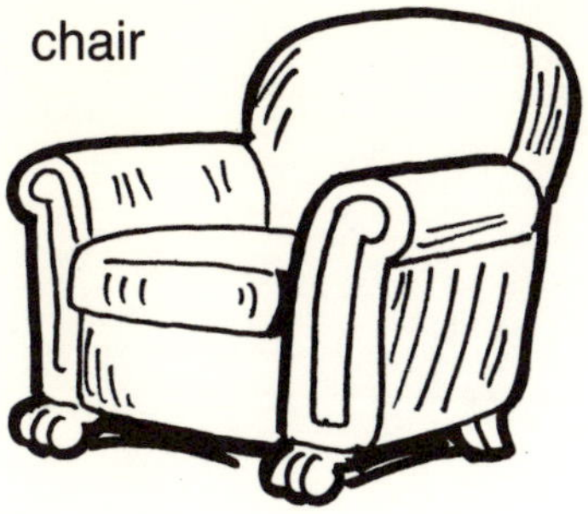

chair

cheese

chick

church

cherries

chipmunk

cl blend

clouds

clock

clown

cr blend

crayons

crown

cross

crab

crib

crackers

donut

duck

dog

dominoes

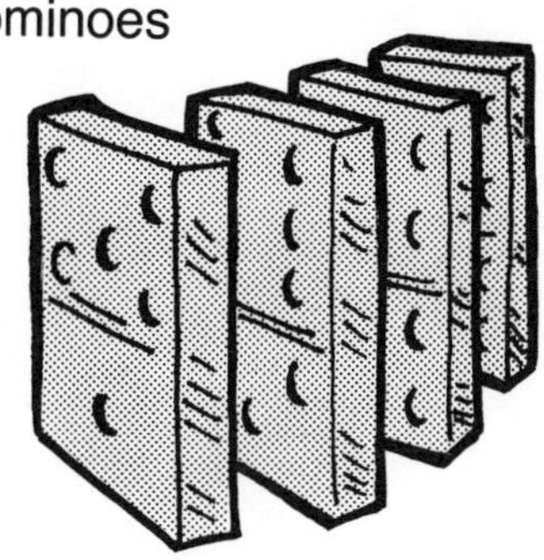

doll

deer

door

dice

dinosaur

desk

---

dr blend

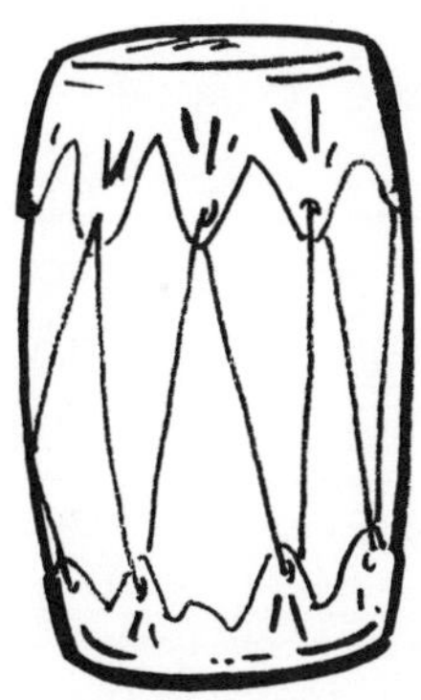

drum

dress

dragon

drop

short e

bed

sled

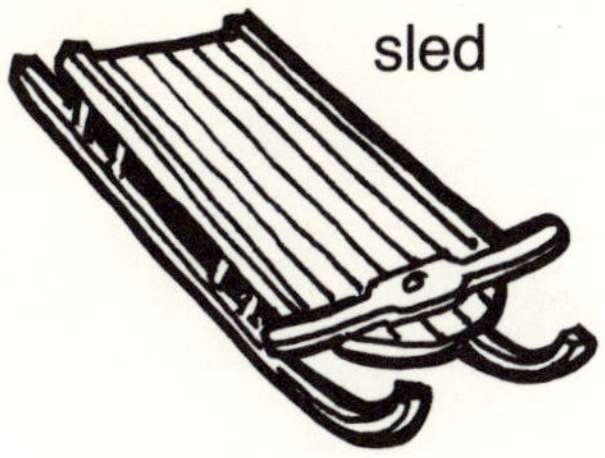

hen

nest

tent

eggs

pen

check

long e and ee

zebra

bee

tree

needle

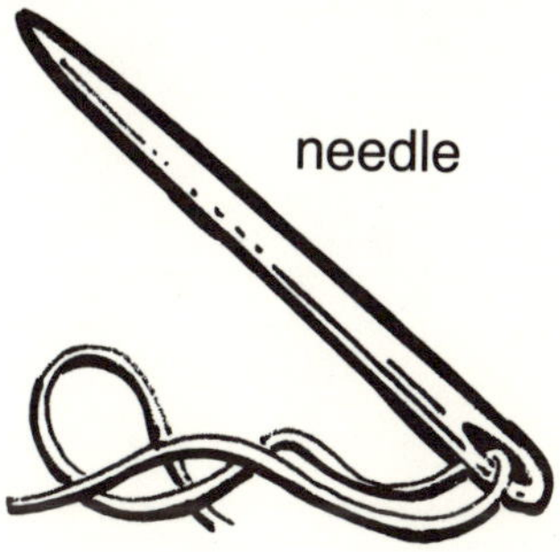

wheel

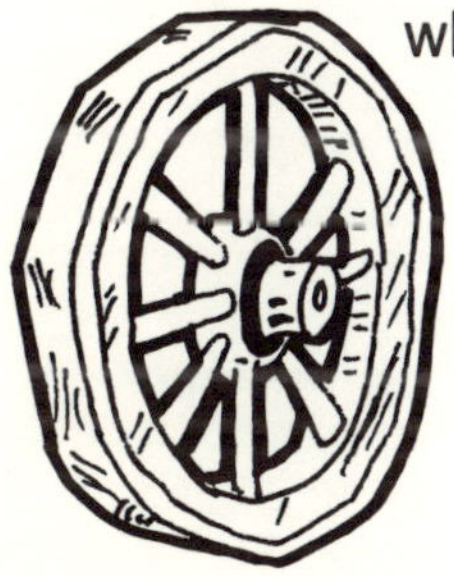

sheep

tweet

ea (long e sound)

seal

beads

peas

leaf

er (vowel with r)

mermaid

thermos

tiger

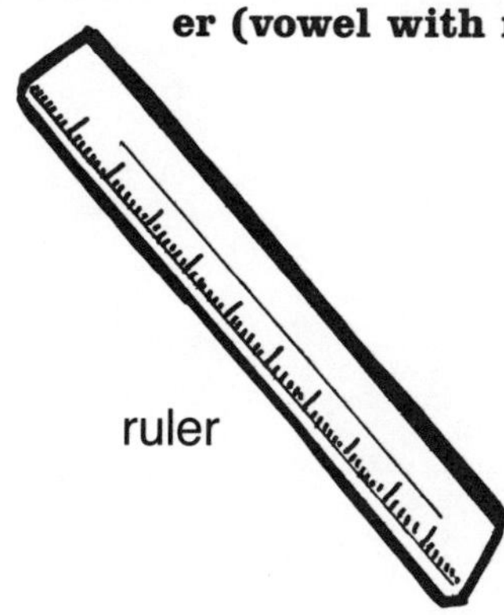

ruler

ea (short e sound)

bread

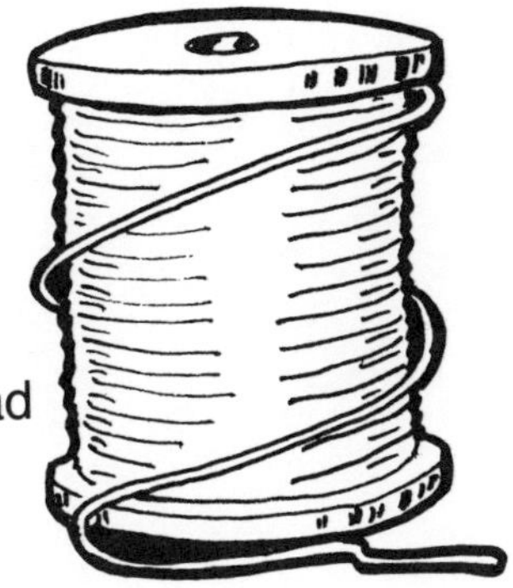

thread

sweater

feather

ew (long u sound)

jewels

stew

screws

ei (long a sound)

eight

weight

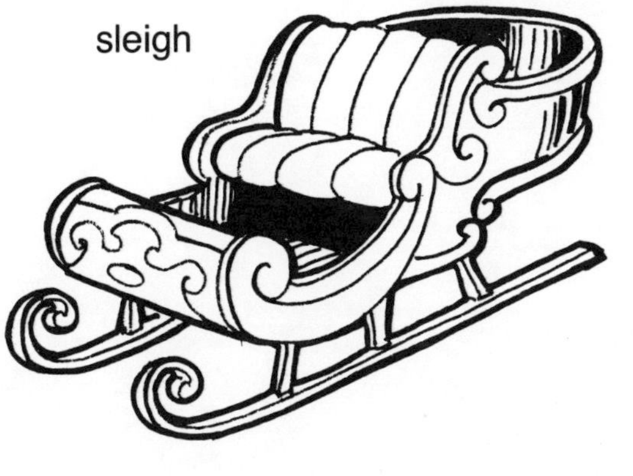

sleigh

initial f

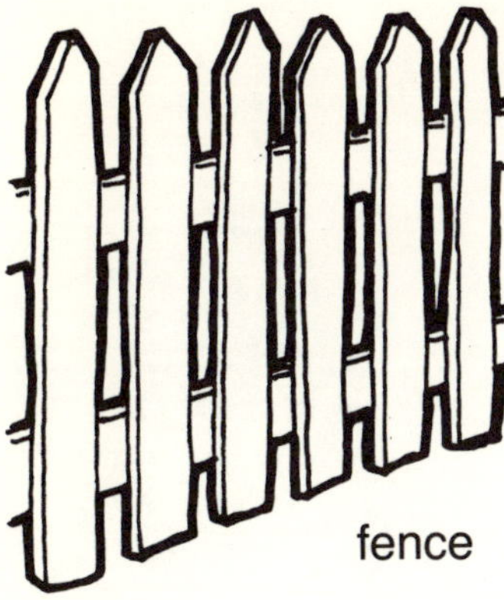

fence

fork

fish

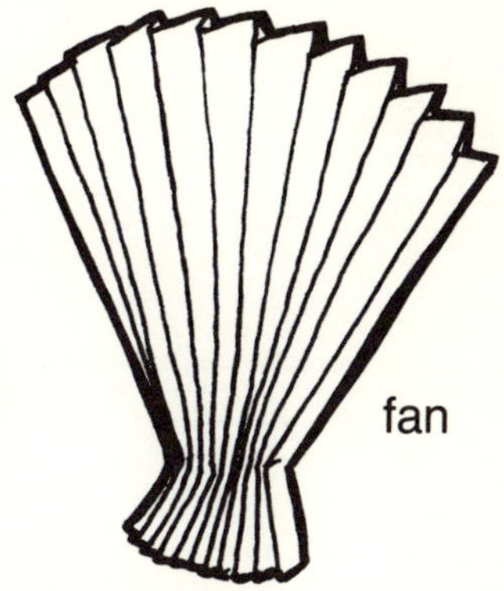

fan

fire engine

fireplace

fox

fl blend

flower

flag

fly

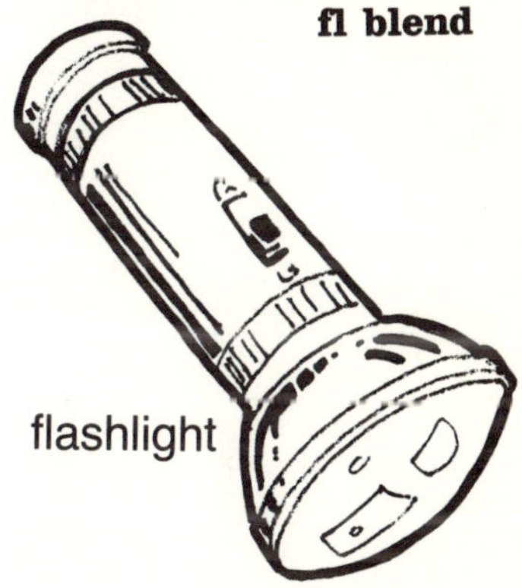

flashlight

fr blend

frog

fruit

French fries

initial hard g

girl

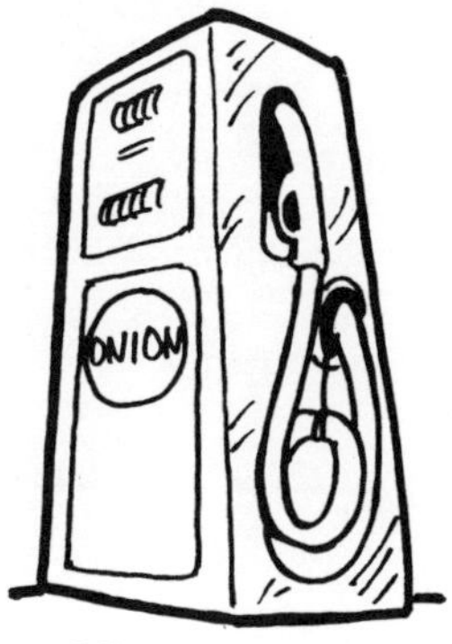
gas

ghost

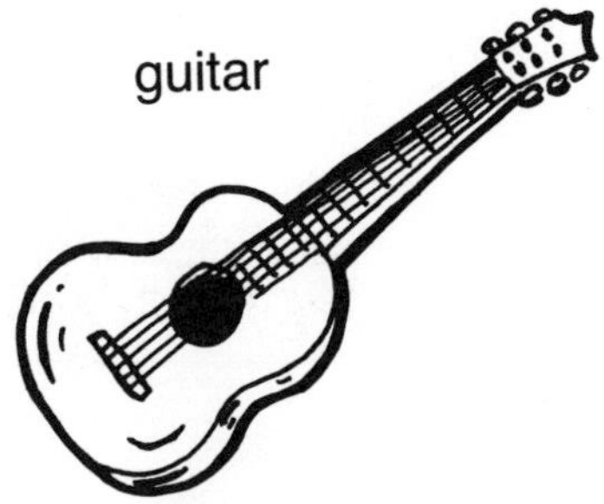
guitar

gum

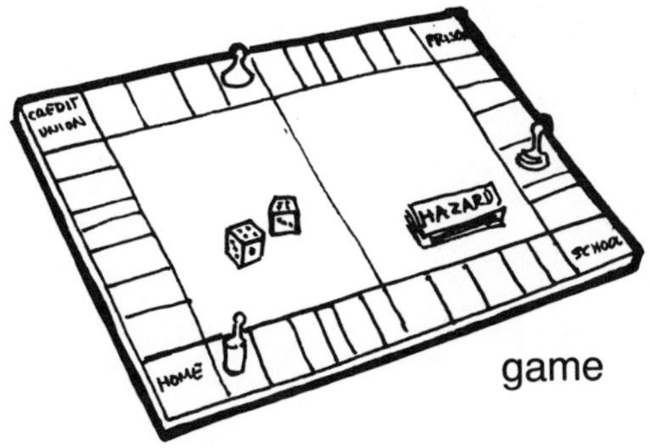
game

goat

initial soft g

gymnast

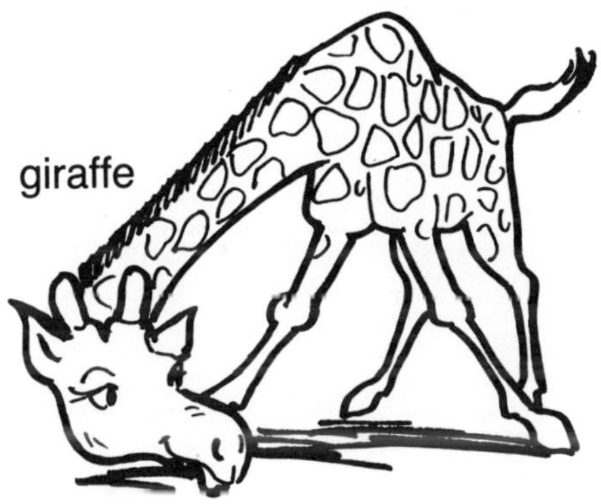
giraffe

gingerbread man

gl blend

glass

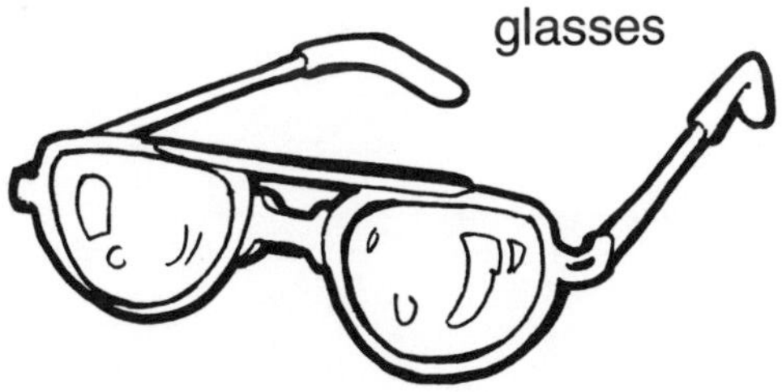
glasses

gloves

gr blend

grapes

grasshopper

greyhound

initial h

house

horse

hammer

heart

hat

hands

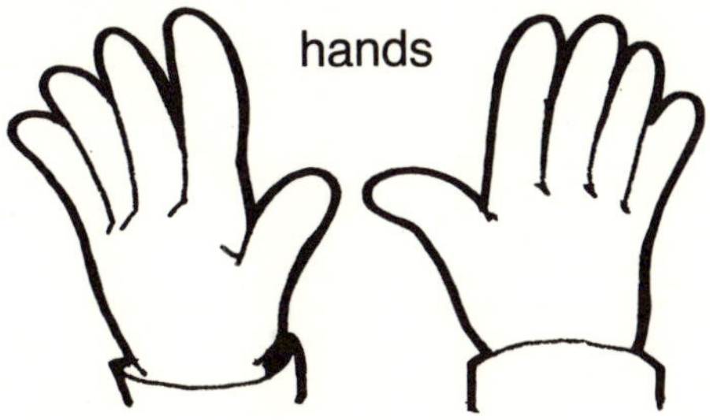

hippo

short i

igloo

pig

ship

king

ring

witch

long i

lion

spider

tiger

long i (final e and ie)

bike

kite

mice

five

knife

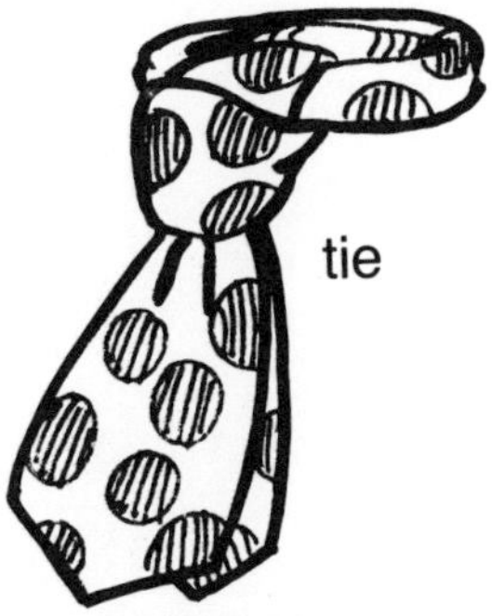

tie

pie

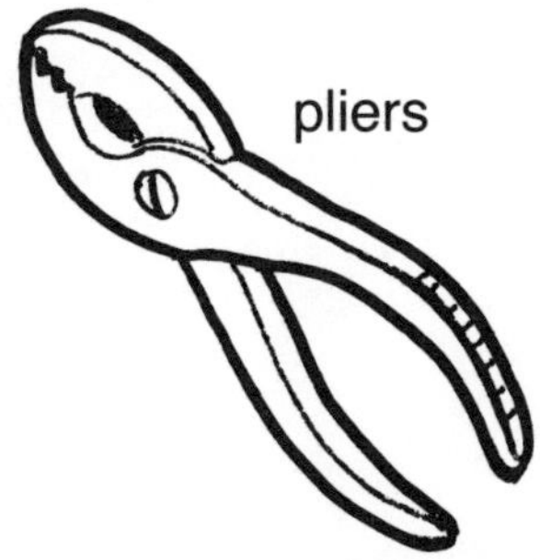

pliers

long i (r-modified)

fire

tire

wires

ir (vowel with r)

t-shirt

bird

skirt

girl

squirrel

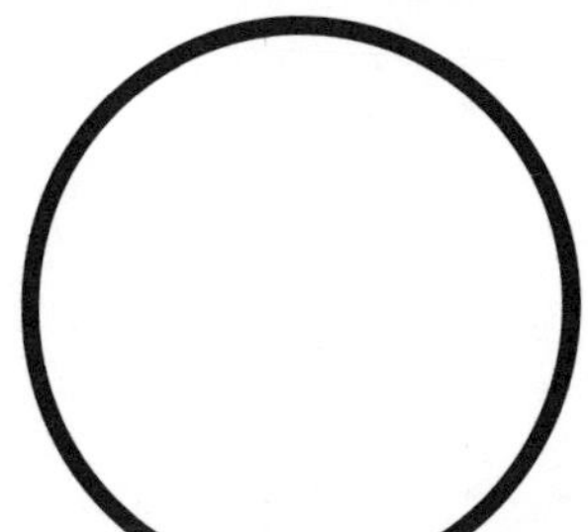

circle

initial j

jar

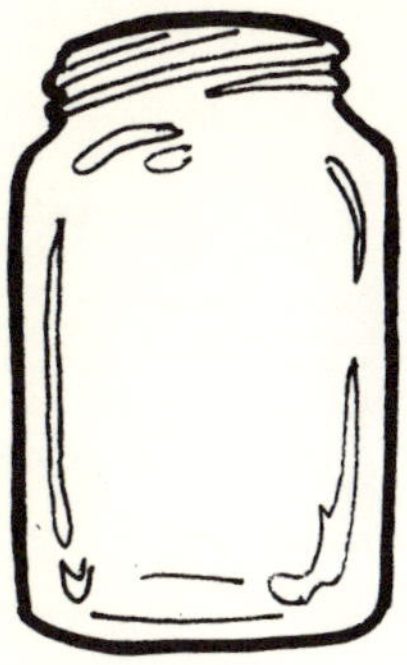

jack-in-the-box

juggler

jumprope

initial k

king

key

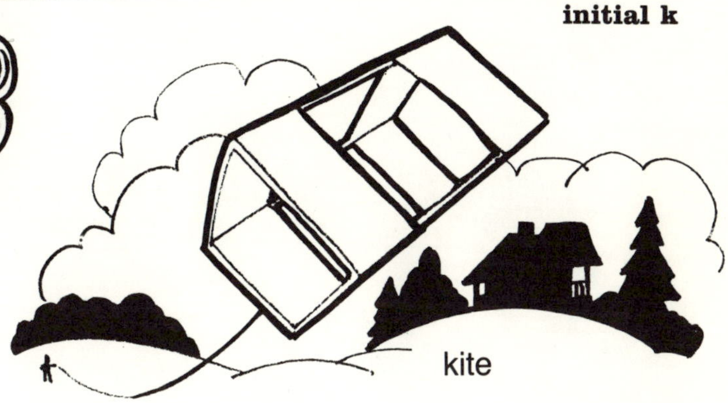

kite

kangaroo

koala

kitchen

initial l

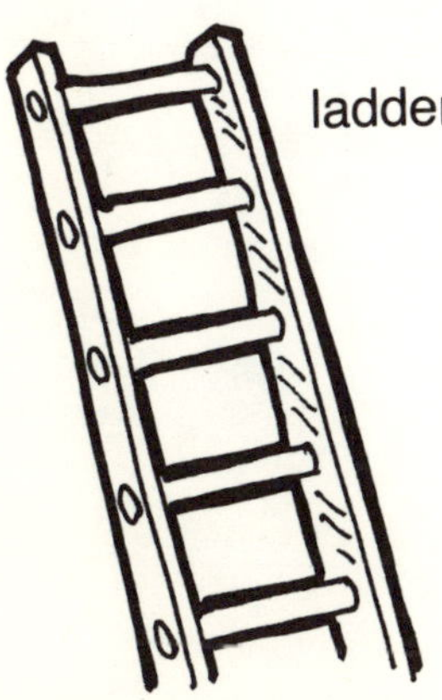

ladder

lion

leaf

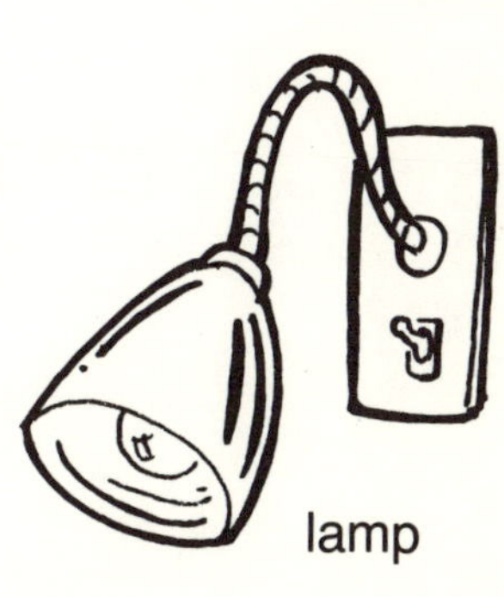

lamp

initial m

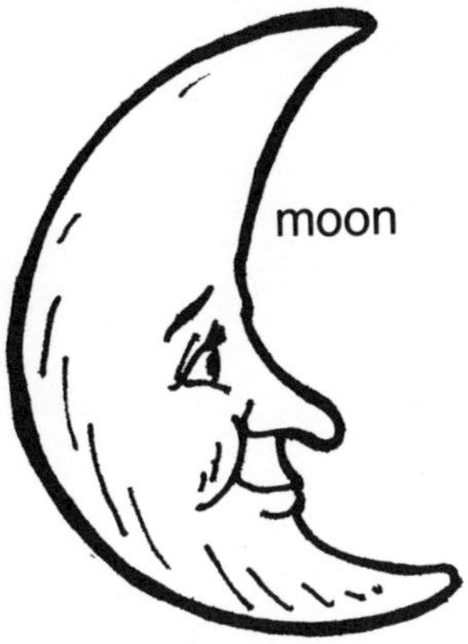

moon

mushroom

monkey

matches

mask

mittens

mouse

money

---

initial n

nest

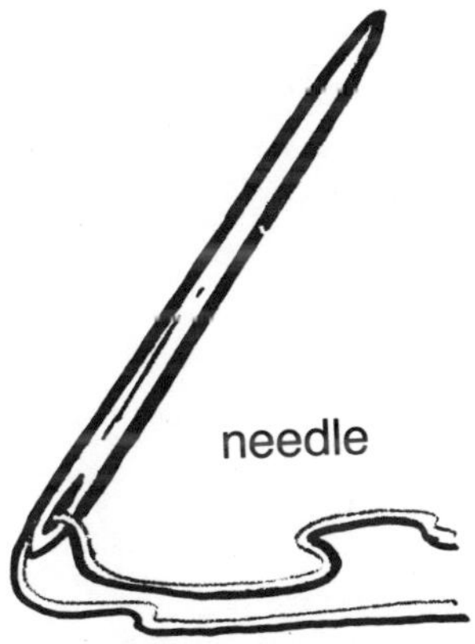

needle

newspaper

nickel

nutcracker

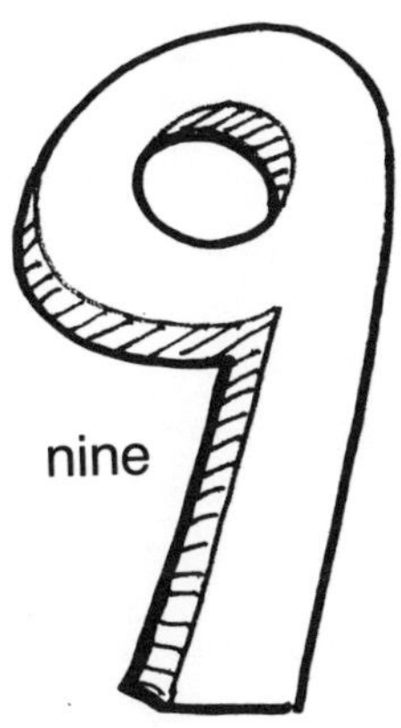

nine

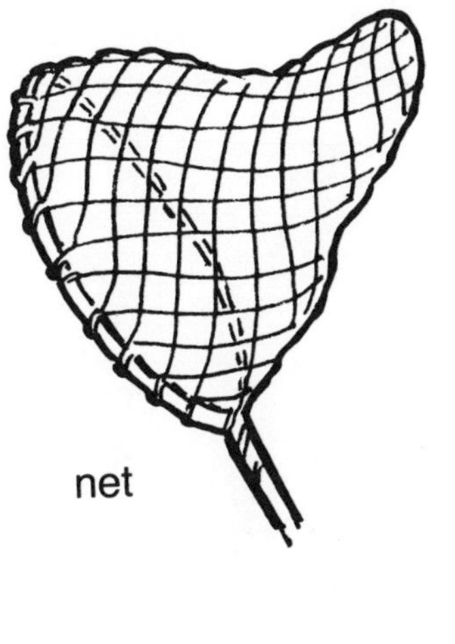

net

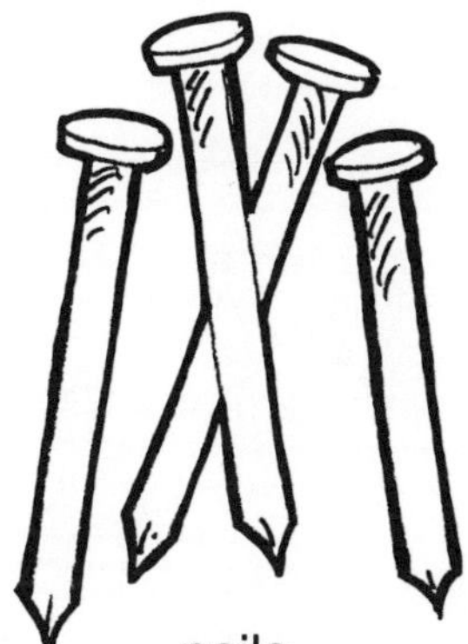

nails

short o

octopus

box

sock

top

clock

fox

mop

doll

long o
(final e signal)

cone

note

phone

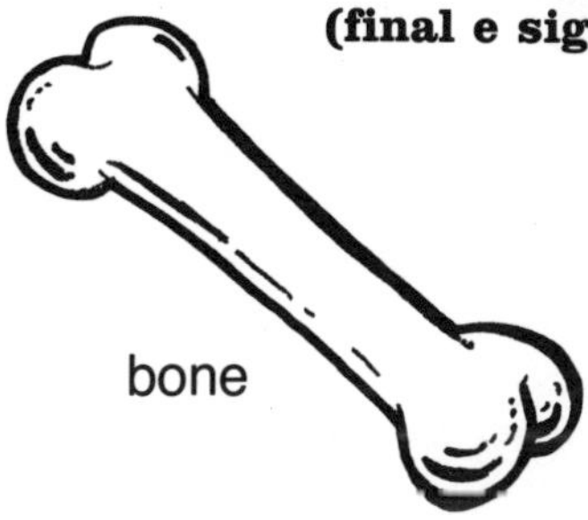

bone

rope

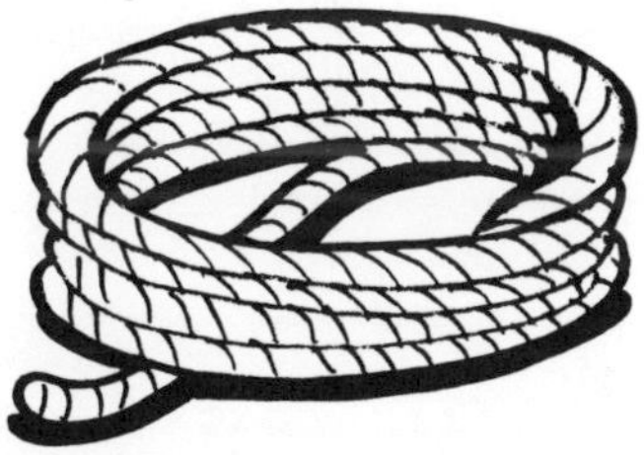

hose

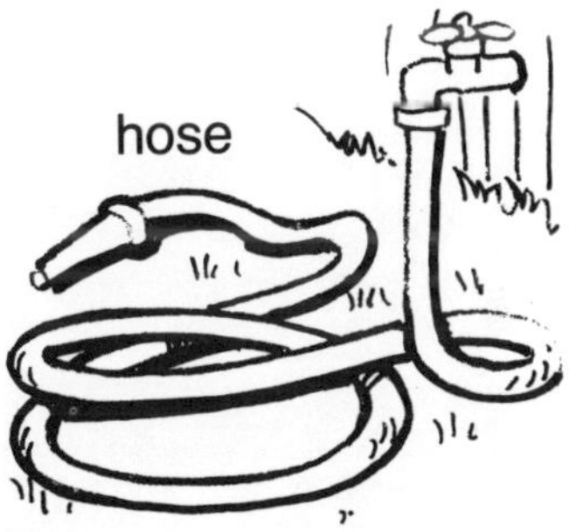

rose

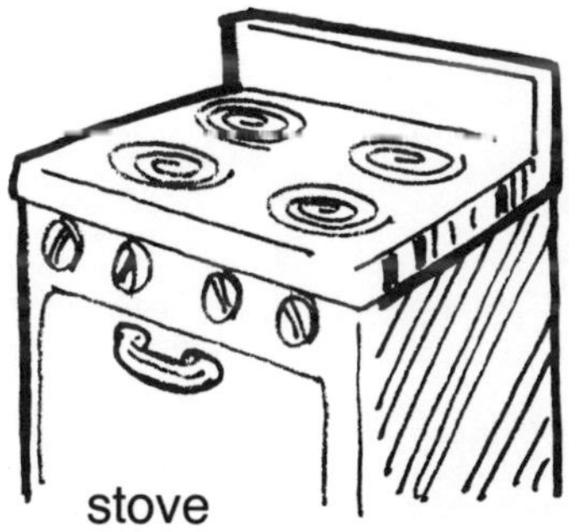

stove

long o

yo-yo

colt

rolls

clover

or (vowel with r)

horn

corn

horse

core

fort

fork

cork

stork

wor

worm

world

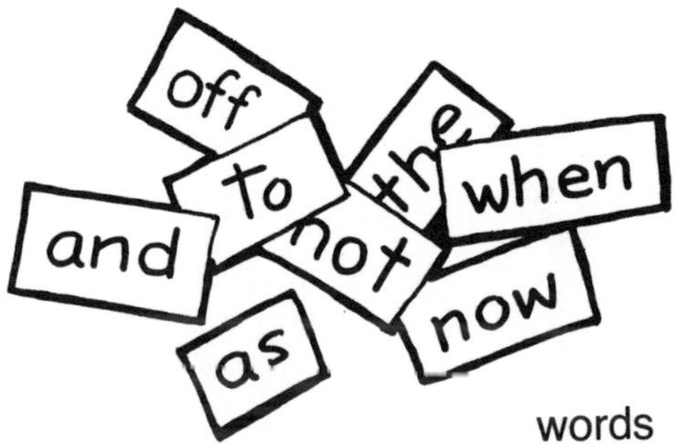

words

ow (long o sound)

bowl

window

arrow

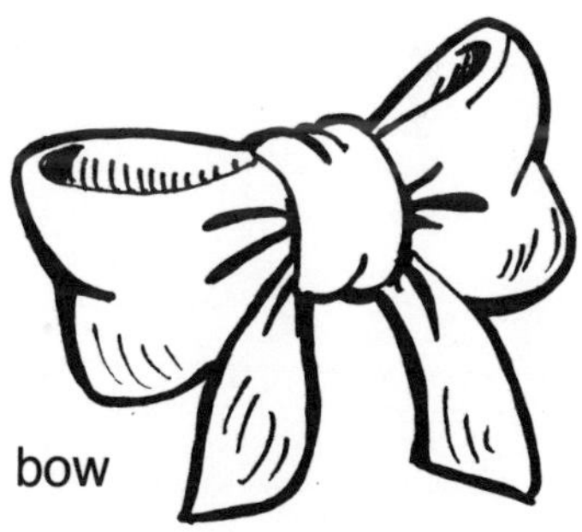

bow

snowman

mower

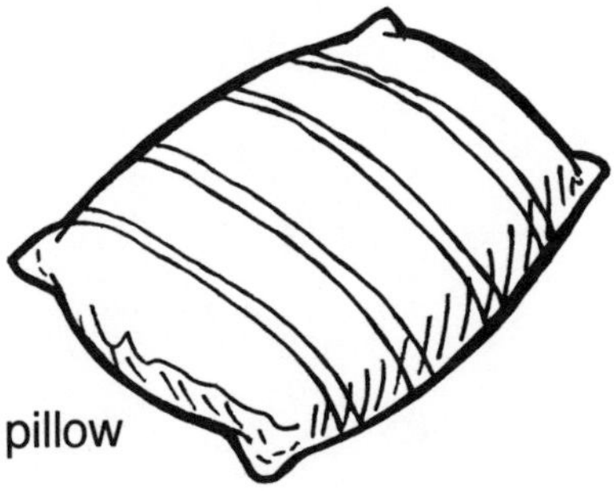

pillow

ow (vowel diphthong)

crown

clown

owl

flower

cow

towel

shower

bow-wow

---

ou (vowel diphthong)

house

mouse

cloud

blouse

---

oi (vowel diphthong)

boil

coins

oink

toys

boy

oysters

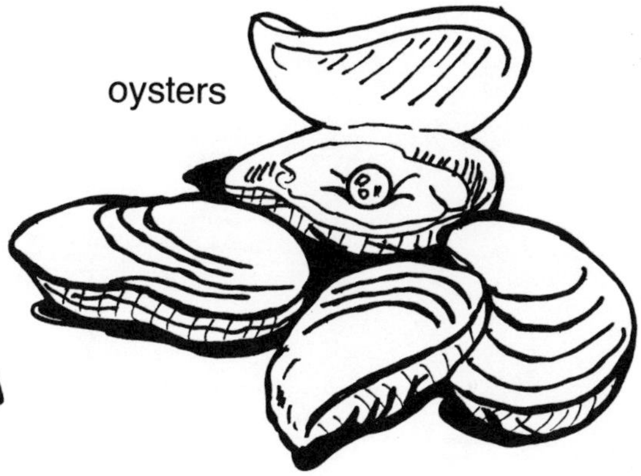

---

oo (long u sound)

spoon

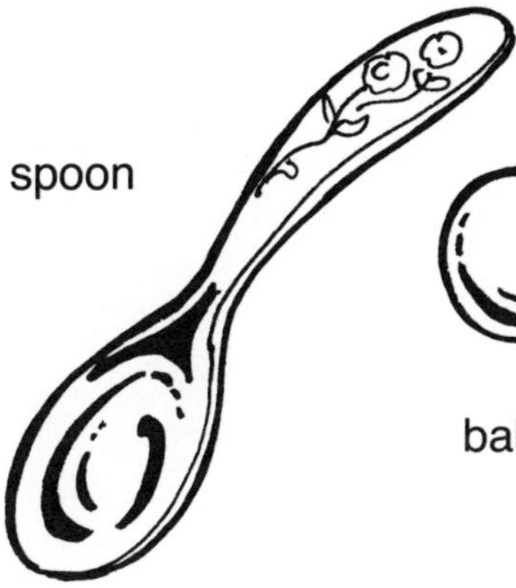

balloon

boots

broom

rooster

raccoon

stool

moo

---

oo (vowel digraph)

wood

cook

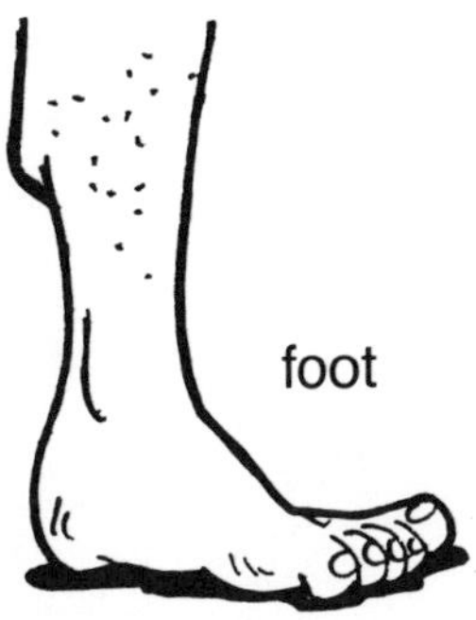

foot

book

oa (long o sound)

toaster

boat

soap

goat

coat

roar

o (schwa sound)

gloves

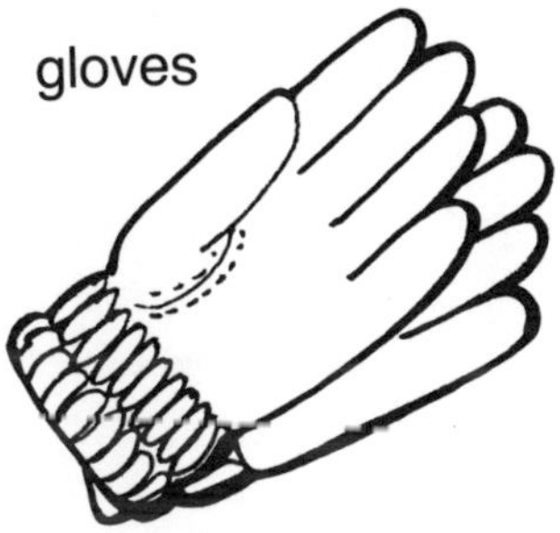

money

honey

shovel

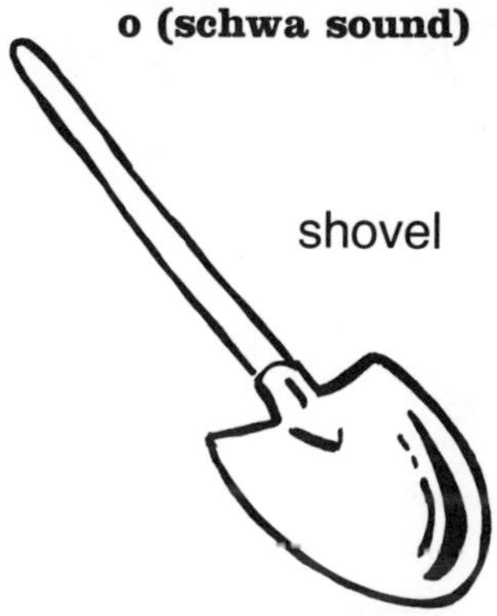

initial p

parrot

pencil

pin

pie

panda

pumpkin

penguin

puppet

pl blend

plant

plate

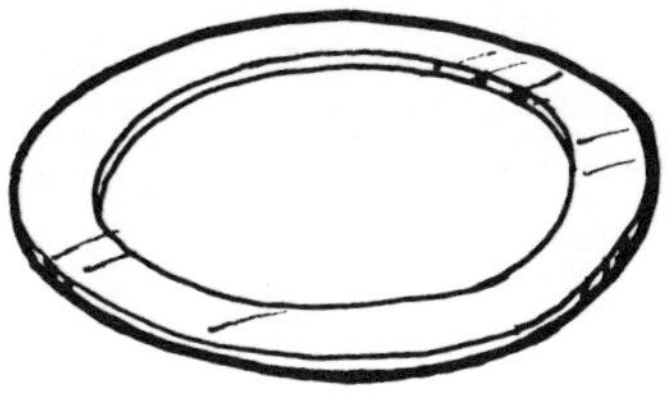

plug

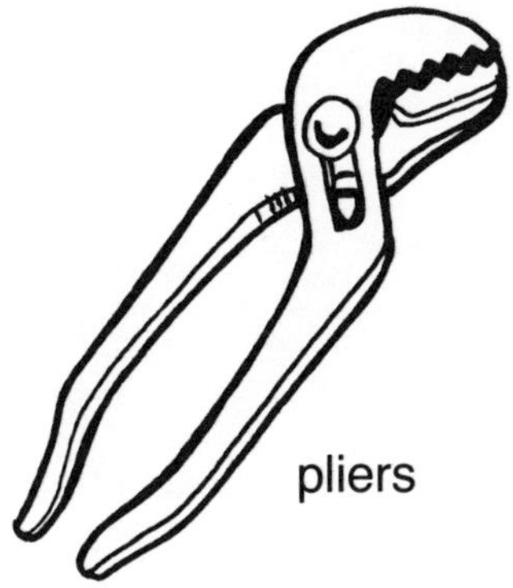

pliers

pr blend

pretzel

present

price tag

qu digraph

quail

queen

quilt

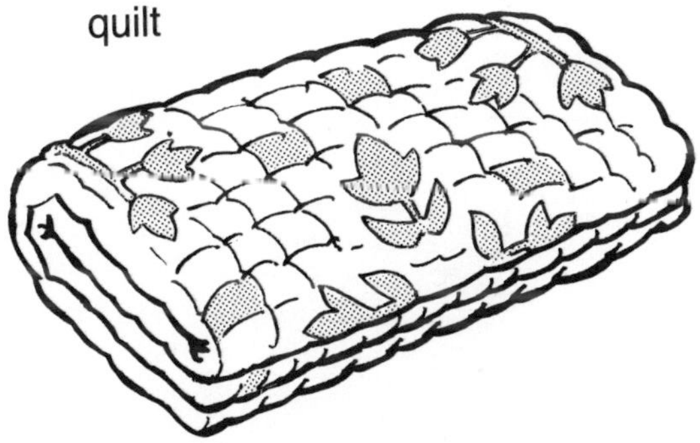

quarter

question mark

quote marks

quart

rabbit

radio

rocket

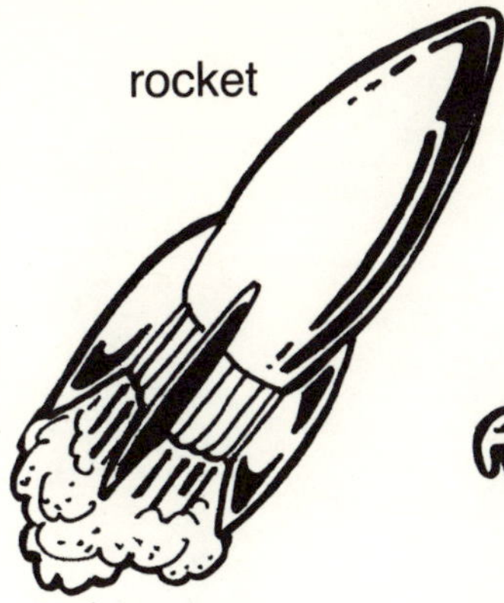

rake

rhinoceros

records

rooster

sun

socks

seal

sandwich

saw

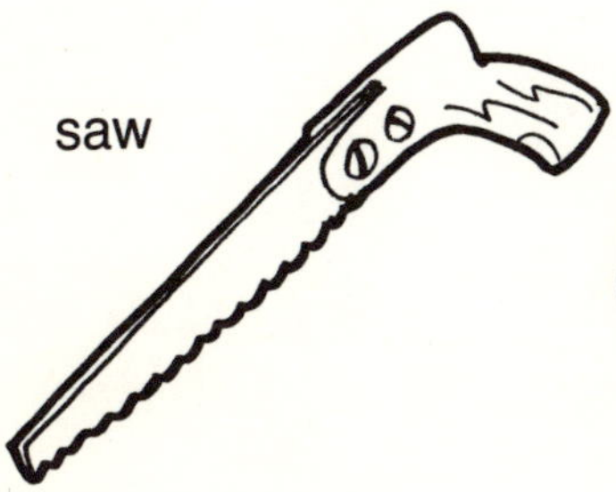

soap

seeds

submarine

sh digraph

ship

shovel

sheep

shells

shirt

shark

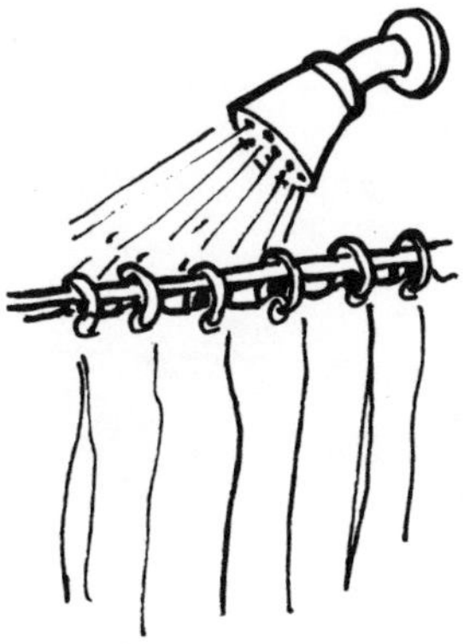

shower

shoes

sc blend

scarecrow

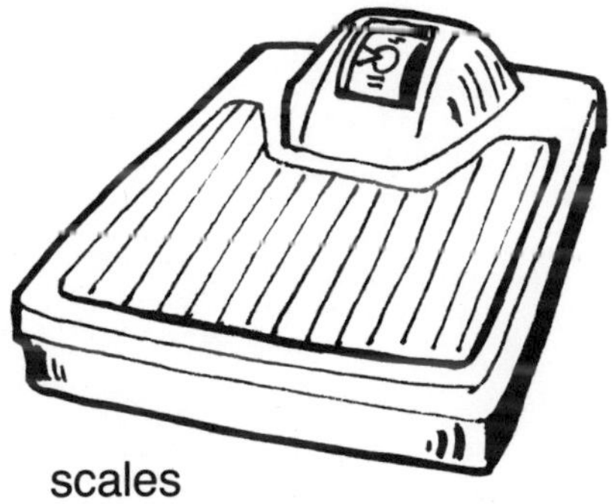

scales

scarf

sk blend

skunk

skates

skis

sl blend

slide

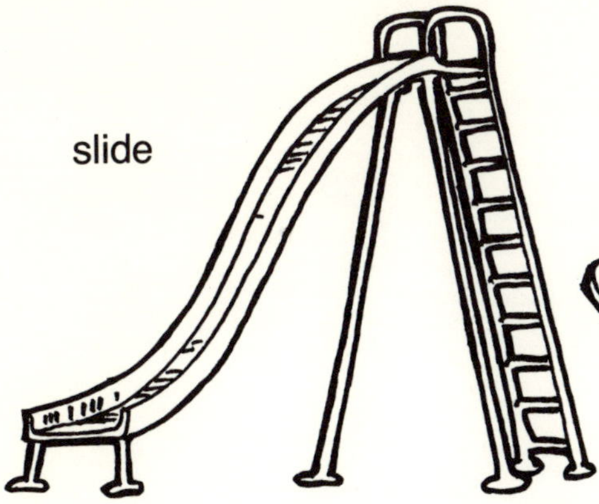

slippers

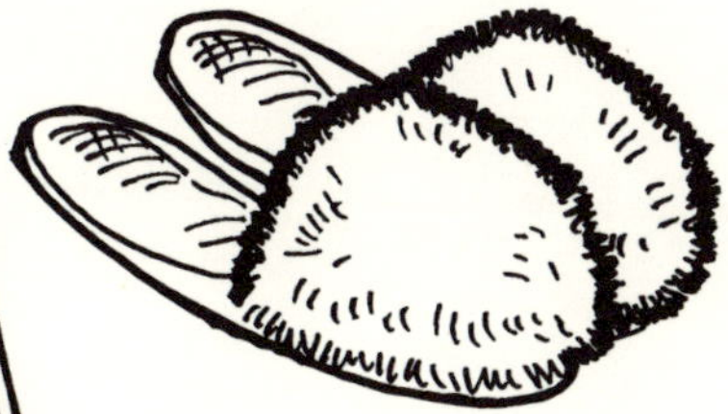

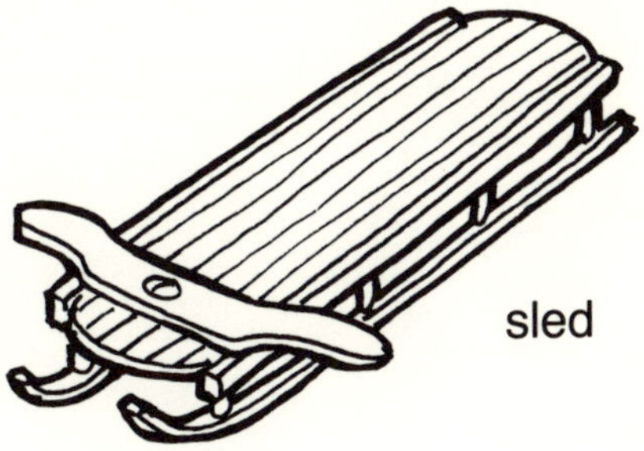

sled

sm blend

smoke

smile

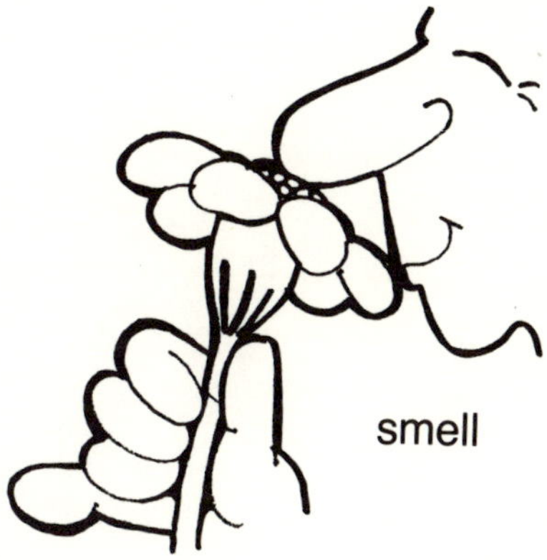

smell

sn blend

snail

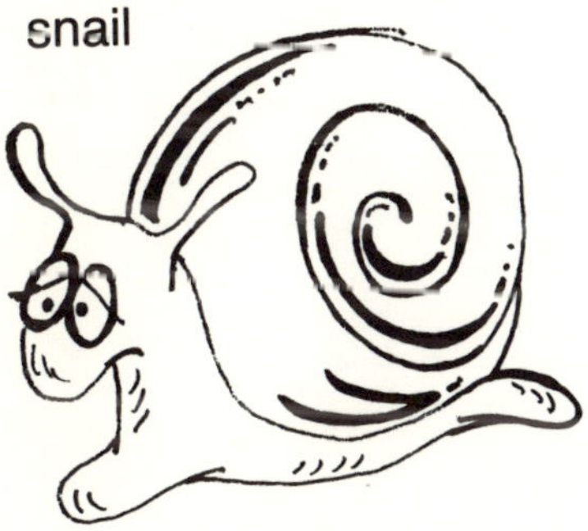

snowflake

snake

sp blend

spoon

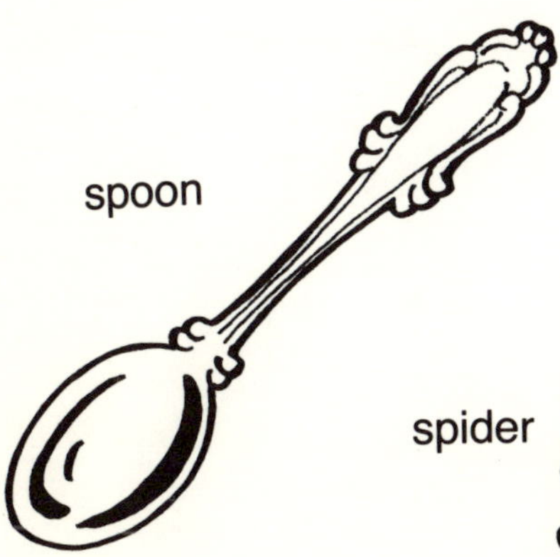

spider

spaghetti

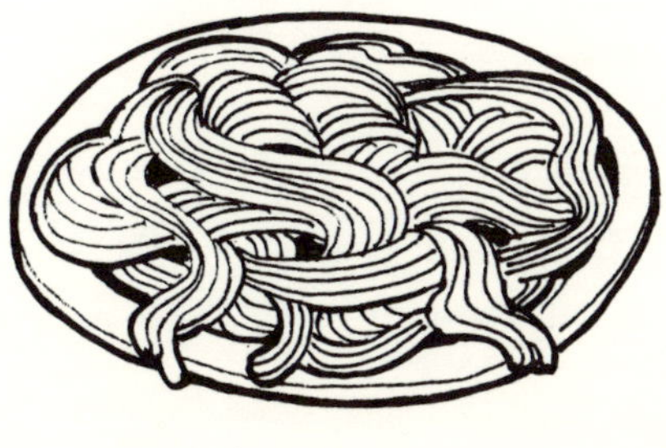

st blend

star

stamp

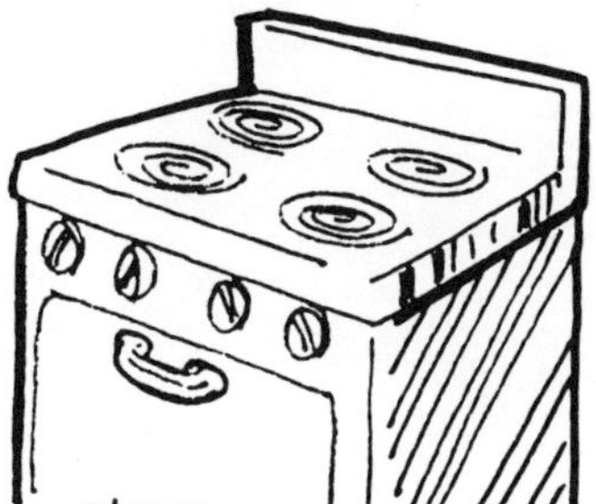

stove

statue

sw blend

swing

sweater

swan

str blend

strawberry

stripes

string

squ blend

squirrel

square

squeak

table

turkey

television

turtle

tent

toothbrush

tiger

toaster

---

th digraph

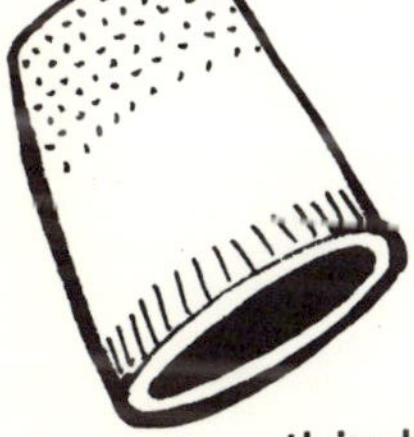

thimble

thirteen

thumb

thorns

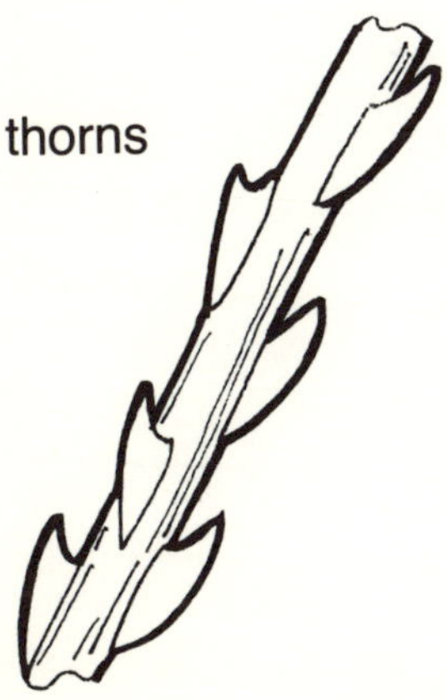

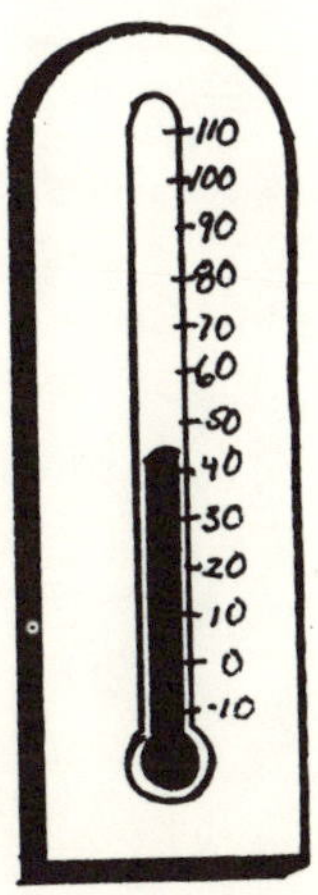

thermometer

thirty

tr blend

tree

truck

triangle

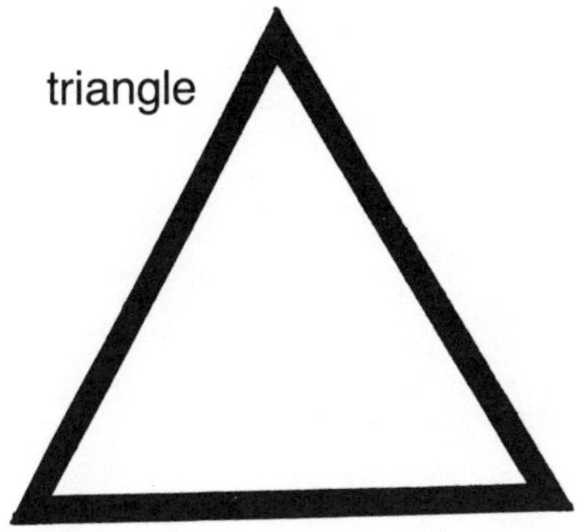

tractor

tracks

trunk

tw blend

twelve

twins

tweet

thr blend

thread

three

throne

short u

umbrella

bug

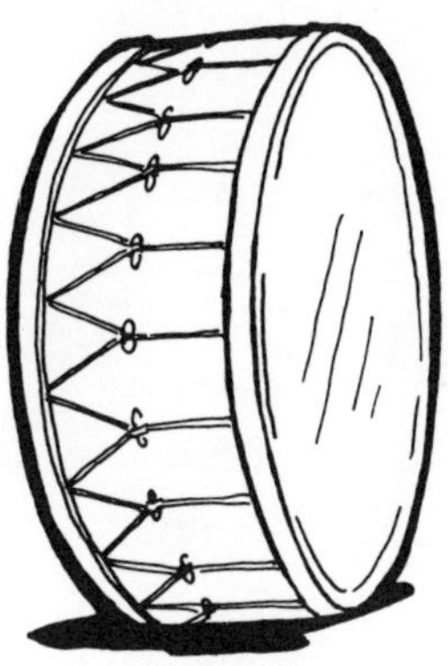

drum

cup

sun

bus

duck

buzz

long u

unicorn

tuba

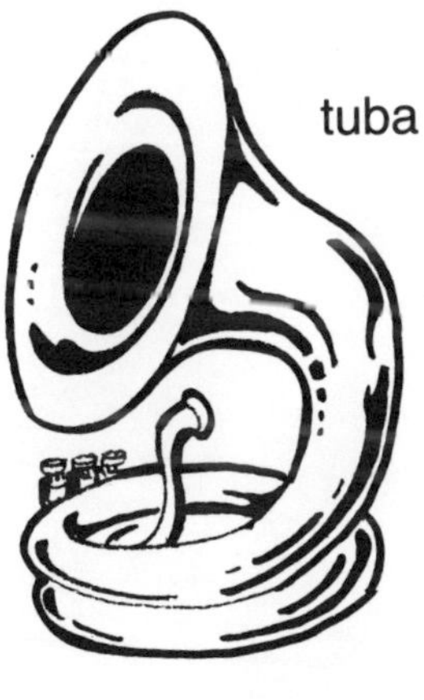

tulips

long u (final e signal)

cube

perfume

tube

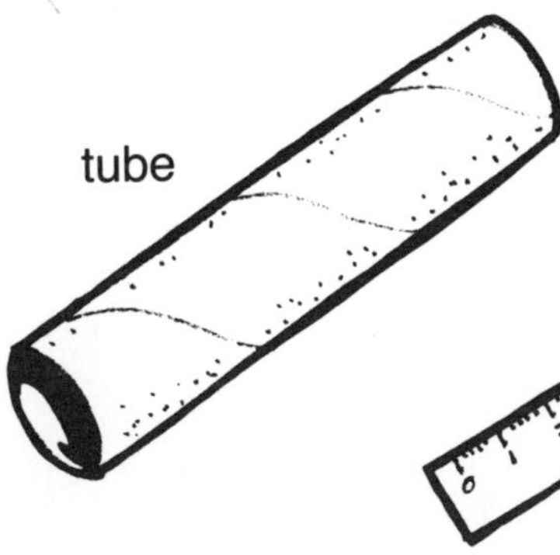

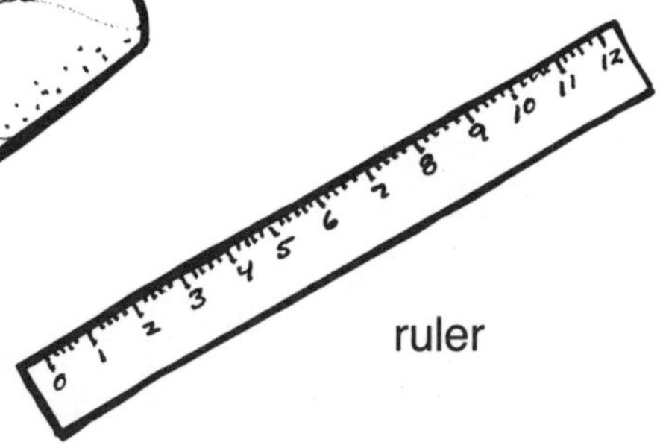

ruler

ur (vowel with r)

church

turtle

purse

turkey

curtains

purr

ui (long u sound)

fruit

suit

suitcase

u (variant vowel)

push pull

bull

bushes

initial v

valentine

vegetables

volcano

vest

initial w

window

wagon

watch

worm

witch

walrus

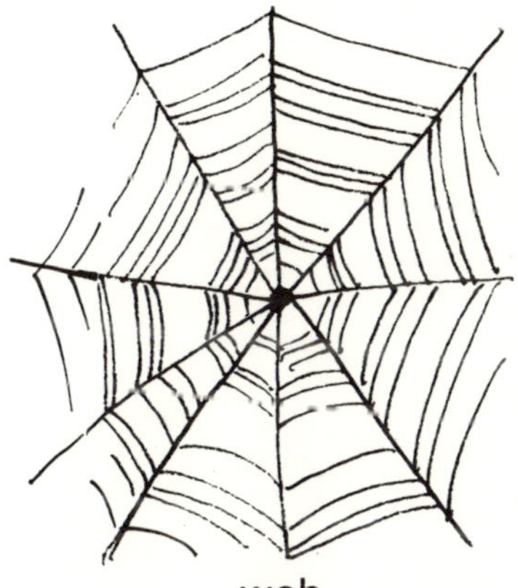
web

wh digraph

whale

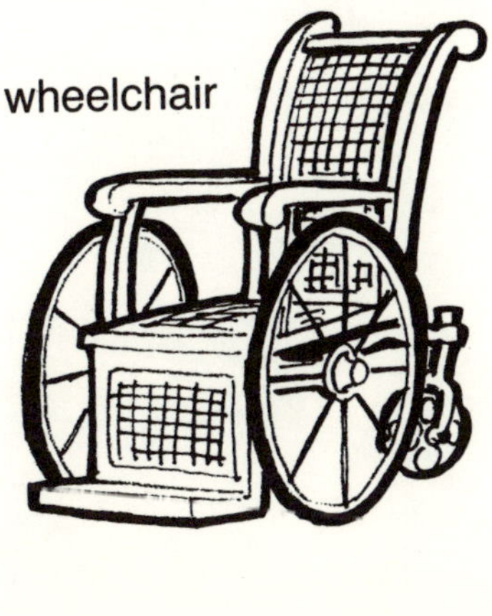
wheelchair

whistle

initial x

x-ray

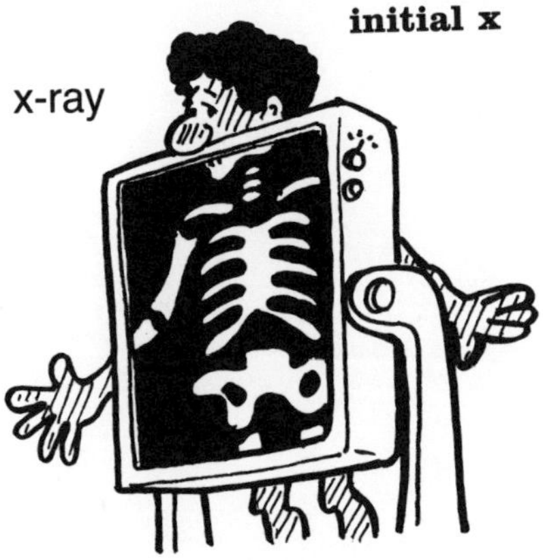

initial y

yo-yo

yarn

final y (long i sound)

fly

cry

sky

final y (long e sound)

penny

candy

fairy

baby

initial z

zipper

zebra

zoo